I Only Have Eyes For You...

PUBLISHED BY MQ PUBLICATIONS LIMITED
12 THE IVORIES, 6—8 NORTHAMPTON STREET
LONDON N1 2HY
TEL: +44 (0) 20 7359 2244
FAX: +44 (0) 20 7359 1616

EMAIL: MAIL@MQPUBLICATIONS.COM
WEBSITE: WWW.MQPUBLICATIONS.COM

COPYRIGHT © 2003 MQ PUBLICATIONS LIMITED
TEXT COMPILATION © 2003 DAVID BAIRD
ARTWORK © 2003 JANET BOLTON

DESIGN: PHILIPPA JARVIS
EDITOR: LEANNE BRYAN

ISBN: 1-84072-601-6

10 9 8 7 6 5 4 3 2 1

PRINTED IN FRANCE BY IMPRIMERIE CLERC

I Only Have Eyes For You...

David Baird

MQP

Are the stars out
tonight?
I don't know if it's
cloudy or bright,
'Cause I only have
eyes for you, dear.

Al Dubin

Twined together and, as is
    customary,
For words of rapture groping, they
"Never such love," swore, "ever
    before was!"
Contrast with all loves that
    had failed or staled

Registered their own as
    love indeed.
Robert Graves

I dare not ask a kiss,
I dare not beg a smile,
Lest having that, or this,
I might grow proud the while.

No, no, the utmost share
Of my desire shall be
Only to kiss that air
That lately kissèd thee.

Robert Herrick

Drink to me only with thine eyes,
And I will pledge with mine;
Or leave a kiss but in the cup
And I'll not look for wine.

Ben Jonson

Put tacks in my shoes,
Feed me vinegar juice,
And do other mean, bad,
   awful stuffsky.
But promise me this:
I won't die without
Kissing my glorious
   Lizzie Pitofsky.

Judith Viorst

In the sweetness of friendship let there be laughter, and sharing of pleasures.

Kahlil Gibran

Love shall be our token;
love be yours and
love be mine.

Christina Rossetti

It is the passion that is in a kiss that gives to it its sweetness; it is the affection in a kiss that sanctifies it.

Christian Nevell Bovee

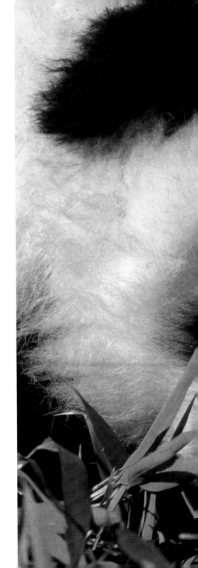

I dream of you to wake;
would that I might
Dream of you and not
wake but slumber on.

Christina Rossetti

Oh, beautiful are the flowers
     of your garden,
The flowers of your garden are fair:
Blue flowers of your eyes
And dusk flower of your hair;
Dew flower of your mouth
And peony-budded breasts,
And the flower of the curve of
     your hand
Where my hand rests.

Helen Hoyt

No man sees far, most see no farther than their noses.

Thomas Carlyle

He took the bride
about the neck
And kissed her lips
with such a
clamorous smack
That at the parting
all the church
did echo.

William Shakespeare

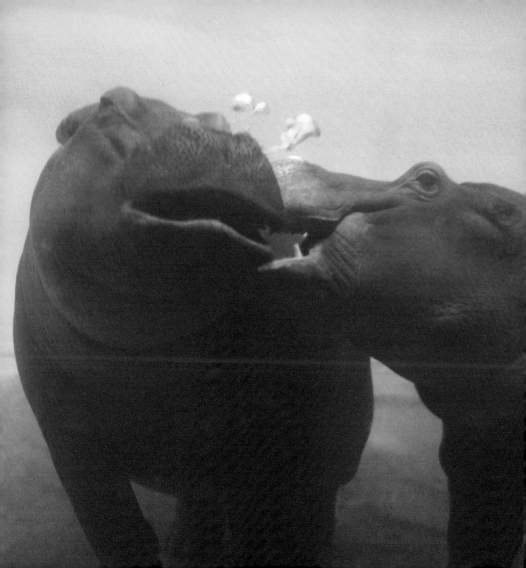

Love means the body, the soul, the life, the entire being. We feel love as we feel the warmth of our blood, we breathe love as we breathe air, we hold it in ourselves as we hold our thoughts. Nothing exists for us.

Guy de Maupassant

29

I have great hopes that
we shall love each other
all our lives as much as if
we had never married at all.

Lord Byron

—All my life I've been waiting for someone, and when I find her, she's a fish. —Nobody said love is perfect.

Tom Hanks and John Candy,
    from "Splash"

I would love to spend all my time writing to you; I'd love to share with you all that goes through my mind, all that weighs on my heart, all that gives air to my soul; phantoms of art, dreams that would be so beautiful if they could come true.

Luigi Pirandello

The eyes are not responsible when the mind does the seeing.

Publilius Syrus

How do I love thee?
   Let me count the ways.
I love thee to the depth
   and breadth and height
My soul can reach…

Elizabeth Barrett Browning

A kiss is a lovely trick designed by nature to stop speech when words become superfluous.

Ingrid Bergman

Oh! Death will find me, long before I tire Of watching you…

Rupert Brooke

False friendship, like the ivy, decays and ruins the walls it embraces; but true friendship gives new life and animation to the object it supports.

Sir Richard Burton

Was this the face that launched a thousand ships, and burnt the topless towers of Ilium?

Christopher Marlowe

If I could write words
Like leaves on an
　　autumn forest floor
What a bonfire my
　　letters would make.
If I could speak words
　　of water
You would drown
　　when I said
"I love you".

Spike Milligan

When, full of warm and eager love,
I clasp you in my fond embrace,
You gently push me back and say,
"Take care, my dear,
    you'll spoil my lace."

William Wetmore Story

Love does not consist in gazing at each other, but in looking outward together in the same direction.

Antoine de Saint-Exupéry

The eyes those silent tongues of love.

Miguel de Cervantes

A kiss, when all is
said, what is it?
A rosy dot placed on
the "i" in loving;
'Tis a secret
Told to the mouth
instead of to the ear.

Edmond Rostand

Oh how sweet it is to hear one's own convictions from another's lips.

Johann Wolfgang von Goethe

And they called it puppy love
Oh, I guess they'll never know
How a young heart really feels
And why I love her so.

Paul Anka

I wonder what fool it was that first invented kissing.

Jonathan Swift

Why does a man take it for granted that a girl who flirts with him wants him to kiss her—when, nine times out of ten, she only wants him to want to kiss her?

Helen Rowland

Reproof on her lips, but a smile in her eyes.

Samuel Lover

In love, there is always
one who kisses and
one who offers the cheek.

French proverb

Come live with me, and be my Love, And we will all the pleasures prove.

Christopher Marlowe

Camerado, I give you
    my hand!
I give you my love more
    precious than money,
I give you myself before
    preaching or law;
Will you give me yourself?

Walt Whitman

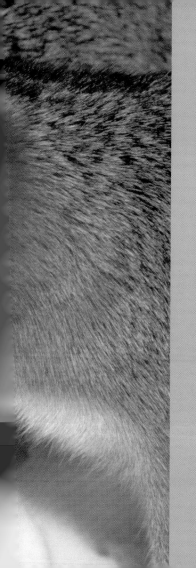

I love him, I love him, ran the patter of her lips
And she formed his name on her tongue and sang.

Carl Sandburg

When love and skill work together, expect a masterpiece.

John Ruskin

...then I did the simplest thing in the world. I leaned down... and kissed him. And the world cracked open.

Agnes de Mille

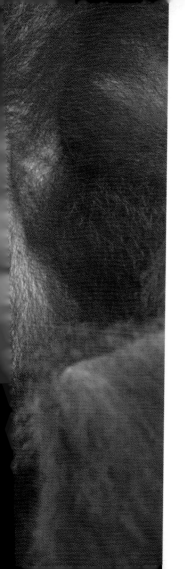

Those whom true love has held, it will go on holding.

Lucius Annaeus Seneca

Come, cuddle your head on my
    shoulder, dear,
Your head like the golden-rod,
And we will go sailing away
    from here
To the beautiful land of Nod.

Ella Wheeler Wilcox

And still they gazed, and
still the wonder grew,
That one small head could
carry all he knew.

Oliver Goldsmith

My heart is a bargain today. Will you take it?

W. C. Fields

If passion drives you, let reason hold the reins.

Benjamin Franklin

'Tis said of love that it sometimes goes, sometimes flies; runs with one, walks gravely with another; turns a third into ice, and sets a fourth in a flame: it wounds one, another it kills: like lightning it begins and ends in the same moment: it makes that fort yield at night which it besieged but in the morning; for there is no force able to resist it.

Miguel de Cervantes

A thing of beauty is a
   joy for ever:
Its loveliness increases;
   it will never
Pass into nothingness;
   but still will keep
A bower quiet for us,
   and a sleep
Full of sweet dreams...

John Keats

Many waters cannot quench love, neither can the floods drown it.

Song of Solomon

Photo Credits